A PARTY FOR CLOUDS

THUNDERSTORMS

Bel the Weather Girl

BELINDA JENSEN

illustrations by Renée Kurilla

series consultant: Lisa Bullard

Ⓜ Millbrook Press/Minneapolis

To my sweet Tori and my one-hundred-pound Bernese mountain dog, Keana, who are snuggled in with me every night we have thunderstorms. You remind me why I want to help kids (and dogs!) understand weather so that it is Not So Scary. —B.J.

For Belinda, Carol, and Emily who saw me as a good fit for this series, even without knowing my appreciation for a good thunderstorm!   —R.K.

Millbrook Press
A division of Lerner Publishing Group, Inc.
241 First Avenue North
Minneapolis, MN 55401 USA

For reading levels and more information, look up this title at www.lernerbooks.com.

Raindrop background: © iStockphoto.com/korinoxe.

Main body text set in ChurchwardSamoa Regular 15/18.
Typeface provided by Chank.

Bel the Weather Girl

Library of Congress Cataloging-in-Publication Data

Jensen, Belinda, author.
    A party for clouds : Thunderstorms / by Belinda Jensen ; Renée Kurilla, illustrator.
        pages cm – (Bel the Weather Girl)
    Includes bibliographical references and index.
    Summary: "Bel and her cousin, Dylan, explore the topic of thunderstorms, learning about thunder, lightning, and how they are formed"–Provided by publisher.
    Audience: 005-007.
    Audience: K to Grade 3.
    ISBN 978-1-4677-7959-3 (lb : alk. paper) – ISBN 978-1-4677-9751-1 (pb : alk. paper) –
ISBN 978-1-4677-9752-8 (eb pdf)
    1. Thunderstorms–Juvenile literature. 2. Severe storms–Juvenile literature. I. Kurilla, Renée, illustrator. II. Title.
QC968.2.J46 2016
551.55'4–dc23   2015016295

Manufactured in the United States of America
1 - CG - 12/31/15

TABLE OF CONTENTS

Chapter One
Flash and Boom!

Bel tiptoed into the kitchen. Her cousin Dylan followed. Snacks would make their sleepover party perfect!

A flash of light lit the room. Thunder rumbled. "Not a thunderstorm!" Dylan said. He ran for the stairs.

Thunderstorms are storms with lightning, thunder, and rain. Thunderstorms become severe when they include high winds and sometimes hail. Most thunderstorms are not severe.

5

Each second, about one hundred bolts of lightning strike somewhere on Earth.

Lightning flashed again. Bel loved to watch storms. But where had Dylan gone? She found him in the tent they'd built in her bedroom.

"You know so much," Dylan said. "If you're really Bel the Weather Girl, why didn't you warn me a storm was coming?"

"It's okay, Dylan," Bel answered. "Thunderstorms happen a lot in the summer. Mom says this isn't a bad one."

Chapter Two
Electricity on the Loose

Bel got into the tent. "We're safe here in the house, Stormy." She gave her dog a big hug. "Let me tell you about lightning and thunder, Dylan. Weather isn't so scary once you understand it!"

Bel continued. "Thunderstorm clouds are called cumulonimbus. Lots of energy builds up in these clouds. The energy is really electricity. And guess what? Electricity makes lightning."

"What about thunder?" Dylan asked. "Stormy and I hate all that noise!"

Lightning can be dangerous. But thunder is helpful. It warns us that lightning is nearby. Remember this safety tip: when thunder roars, go indoors!

"Lightning is hotter than the surface of the sun! The air pulls away from that heat. Then it crashes back together." Bel clapped. "Thunder is just the sound of all that moving air.

"Lightning and thunder happen at the same time. But sound moves slower than light," Bel said. "So we see lightning before we hear thunder."

Bel stepped out of the tent. She grabbed her stuffed chimp. "Come out, Dylan. I'll show you a fun game!"

Thunderstorm safety tips: Go inside a building or car. If you're stuck outside, get away from water. Don't stand under tall objects. Crouch down, but don't lie flat on the ground.

Dylan slowly got out. Bel said, "This is Thunder Chimp. He's going to help us play Thunder Count! This game will let us know when the storm is moving away."

Bel pointed outside. Lightning flashed.
She started counting. "One chimpanzee,
two chimpanzees, three chimpanzees,
four chimpanzees, five chimpanzees."
Then thunder rumbled.

Sometimes you see
lightning but never hear
thunder. That's called
heat lightning. It's too
far away for the sound
to reach you.

14

"I counted five chimpanzees between the lightning and thunder. Five chimpanzees is five seconds," said Bel. "Sound travels about a mile in five seconds. So the storm is one mile away!"

"Hey, let's do that again!" said Dylan. They waited. Then lightning flashed. They counted together. This time they got to seven chimpanzees. Then

BOOM!

"What does seven mean?" asked Dylan.

"Seven is more than a mile. The storm is moving away!" said Bel.

Bel's mom came into the room. "The storm is quieting down. You two should quiet down too! There's way too much energy and noise at this party."

Lightning can strike 10 miles (16 km) away from a storm. Stay inside for thirty minutes after you hear thunder.

Bel the Weather Girl

As they settled down to sleep, Dylan laughed. "Thunderstorms are just cloud parties. They're full of energy and noise. That's not so scary! Next storm, I'll try Thunder Count with my crocodile."

Chapter Four

The Party Is Over

In the morning, Bel and Dylan ate their breakfast outside. "The cloud party is over," said Dylan.

Bel looked up at the sky. "No thunderstorms for us today. But stay tuned for tomorrow.

Because every day is another weather day!"

Try It: Make a Thunder Bag

There is an easy way for you to see how moving air makes sound—much in the same way that moving air makes the sound of thunder!

Here are the steps to follow:

1. Take a brown paper lunch bag. Fill it with air by blowing into it.

2. Twist the open end closed. Hold it with one hand.

3. Pop the bag like a balloon by smashing your other hand into it.

Bang! The air inside the bag rushes out. It pushes away the air outside the bag. The air keeps moving. It makes a loud sound when it reaches your ears.

1

2

3

POP!

Glossary

cumulonimbus: a high-towering cloud that often produces rain and storms

electricity: a form of energy that is found in nature or can be produced

energy: usable power

heat lightning: lightning that is far enough away that you can't hear thunder

lightning: a flash of light created by electricity in a thunderstorm

severe: very great or intense

thunder: the loud sound created when lightning causes air to move

thunderstorm: a storm with lightning and thunder

Further Reading

Books

Bodden, Valerie. *Thunderstorms*. Mankato, MN: Creative Education, 2012.
Learn more about thunderstorms by reading and looking at the colorful photographs in this book.

Geisert, Arthur. *Thunderstorm*. New York: Enchanted Lion, 2013.
Follow along with a timeline and pictures as a farm family experiences a thunderstorm.

Stiefel, Chana. *Thunderstorms*. New York: Children's Press, 2009.
This book will teach you many more facts about thunderstorms. Enter your zip code and see weather forecasts in your area for today and tomorrow.

Websites

KidsHealth: Thunderstorms
http://kidshealth.org/kid/watch/out/thunderstorms.html
This website has some good tips for things you can do if you're afraid of thunderstorms.

Leon the Lion's Lightning Safety Game
http://www.lightningsafety.noaa.gov/multimedia/Lightning_Game.swf
Play a game from the National Oceanic and Atmospheric Administration to help you learn when you are safe or not safe during a thunderstorm.

Lightning
http://www.nws.noaa.gov/om/brochures/owlie-lightning.pdf
Download this booklet from the National Weather Service and color in the pages yourself while learning more about lightning.

Index

LERNER
e
SOURCE

Expand learning beyond the printed book. Download free, complementary educational resources for this book from our website, www.lerneresource.com.